ANTHOLOGY OF ROMANTIC MUSIC

By the same author

Romantic Music: A History of Musical Style in Nineteenth-Century Europe

The Norton Introduction to Music History

Anthology of
ROMANTIC MUSIC

LEON PLANTINGA, EDITOR

Yale University

W · W · NORTON & COMPANY

New York · London

Manufacturing by The Maple-Vail Book Group.
Jacket painting, *Music Party* by J. M. W. Turner courtesy
The Tate Gallery, London

First Edition

Library of Congress Cataloging in Publication Data
Main entry under title:
Anthology of romantic music.
   (The Norton introduction to music history)
Designed to accompany Romantic music
by Leon Plantinga.
   1. Musical analysis—Music collections.   2. Music
appreciation—Music collections.   3. Instrumental
music—19th century.   4. Vocal music—19th century.
I. Plantinga, Leon.   II. Plantinga, Leon.   Romantic
music.   III. Title.   IV. Series.
MT6.5.A59   1984   83-42652

ISBN 0-393-01811-3
ISBN 0-393-95211-8 (pbk.)

W. W. Norton & Company, Inc., 500 Fifth Avenue, New
York, N. Y. 10110
W. W. Norton & Company, Ltd., 37 Great Russell Street,
London WC1B 3NU

1 2 3 4 5 6 7 8 9 0

Contents

Preface

This anthology is intended as a companion volume to my *Romantic Music: a History of Musical Style in Nineteenth-Century Europe* (New York, W. W. Norton, 1984), which presents rather extended discussions of many of the compositions included here. It is also hoped, however, that the present volume will be of independent use simply as a convenient collection of study-scores for students of nineteenth-century music. To that end an attempt has been made to achieve a reasonable balance as to chronology, geographical distribution, and genre. For the most part compositions are presented entire; only in the case of symphonies and operas has it been necessary to offer extracts—movements or scenes—rather than whole works. And for selections from opera and oratorio, limitations of space have dictated the use of piano-vocal reductions instead of full scores.

Several people have helped me prepare this anthology; foremost among them are Judith Silber, who gave me good advice and saw to countless details; Jane Baun, who transliterated the Russian texts; and Claire Brook and Susan Zurn at W. W. Norton, who have shepherded it through the complexities of publication.

Leon Plantinga
New Haven, Conn.
May, 1984

1

LUDWIG VAN BEETHOVEN (1770–1827)
Piano Sonata No. 17 in D Minor, Opus 31, No. 2 (1802)

2

BEETHOVEN
Symphony No. 3 in E♭ Major ("Eroica"), Opus 55 (1803), first movement

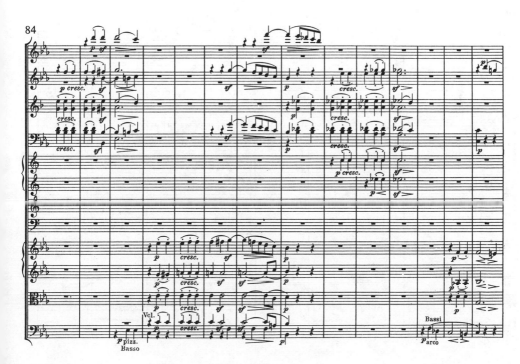

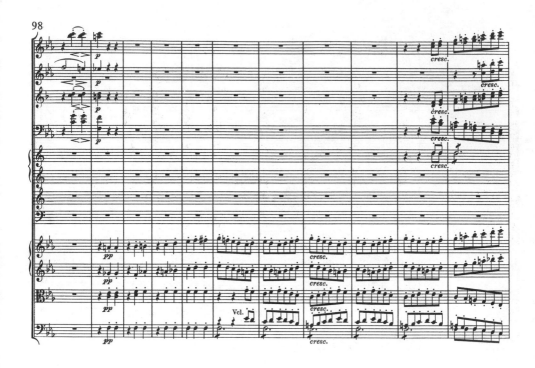

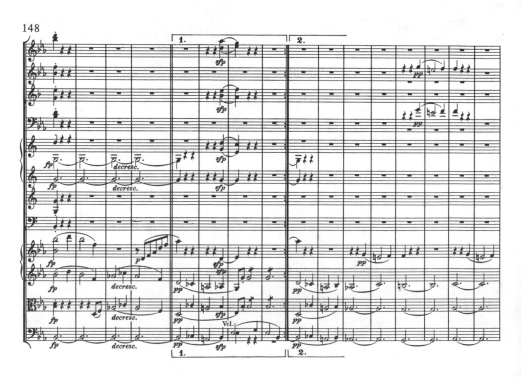

215

222

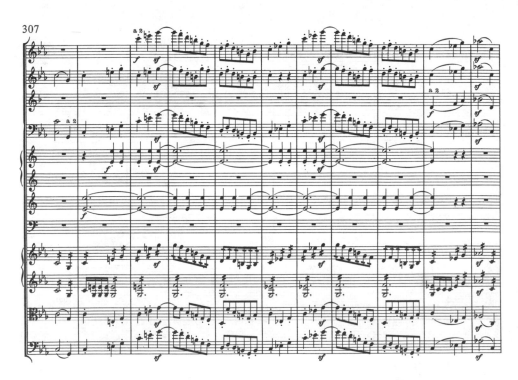

364

378

394

410

425

436

469

477

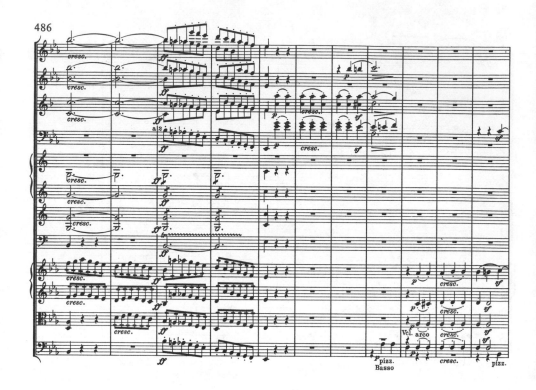

574

584

637

646

674

683

3

BEETHOVEN
String Quartet in C♯ Minor, Opus 131 (1826)

N⁰ 4. Andante ma non troppo e molto cantabile.

4

FRANZ SCHUBERT (1797–1828)
Quintet in A Major for Piano and Strings
("The Trout"), D.667 (1819),
fourth and fifth movements

5

JAN LADISLAV DUSÍK (1760–1812)
Piano Sonata No. 24, Opus 61 (1806–07)

*) ossia [musical notation] etc.

6a

SCHUBERT
Gretchen am Spinnrade, D.118 (1814)

Meine Ruh ist hin,
Mein Herz ist schwer;
Ich finde sie nimmer
Und nimmermehr.

Wo ich ihn nicht hab'
Ist mir das Grab,
Die ganze Welt
Ist mir vergällt.

Mein armer Kopf
Ist mir verrückt,
Mein armer Sinn
Ist mir zerstückt.

Meine Ruh ist hin
Mein Herz ist schwer;
Ich finde sie nimmer
Und nimmermehr.

Nach ihm nur schau' ich
Zum Fenster hinaus,
Nach ihm nur geh' ich
Aus dem Haus.

Sein hoher Gang,
Sein' edle Gestalt,
Seines Mundes Lächeln,
Seiner Augen Gewalt,

Und seiner Rede
Zauberfluss,
Sein Händedruck,
Und ach, sein Kuss!

Meine Ruh ist hin,
Mein Herz ist schwer;
Ich finde sie nimmer
Und nimmermehr.

Mein Busen drängt
Sich nach ihm hin;
Ach, dürft' ich fassen
Und halten ihn

Und küssen ihn,
So wie ich wollt',
An seinen Küssen
Vergehen sollt'!

My peace is gone,
My heart is heavy;
I will find it never
And never again.

Where I do not have him
Is like the grave to me,
The whole world
Is loathsome to me.

My poor head
Is crazed,
My poor wits
Are distracted.

My peace is gone,
My heart is heavy;
I will find it never
And never again.

Only for him I look
Out the window,
Only for him I go
Out of the house.

His superior bearing,
His noble form,
His mouth's smile,
His eyes' power,

And of his talk
The magic flow,
The press of his hand,
And ah, his kiss!

My peace is gone,
My heart is heavy;
I will find it never
And never again.

My bosom yearns
For him;
Ah, would I clasp him
And hold him

And kiss him,
Just as I wanted to,
Under his kisses
I should pass away!

Johann Wolfgang von Goethe   trans. by Leon Plantinga

6b

SCHUBERT
Erlkönig, D.328 (1815)

Wer reitet so spät durch Nacht
und Wind?
Es ist der Vater mit seinem Kind;
Er hat den Knaben wohl in dem
Arm,
Er fasst ihn sicher, er hält ihn
warm.

Mein Sohn, was birgst du so
bang dein Gesicht?
Siehst, Vater, du den Erlkönig
nicht?
Den Erlenkönig mit Kron' und
Schweif?
Mein Sohn, es ist ein Nebelstreif.

"Du liebes Kind, komm, geh mit
mir!
Gar schöne Spiele spiel' ich mit
dir;
Manch bunte Blumen sind an
dem Strand;
Meine Mutter hat manch gülden
Gewand."

Mein Vater, mein Vater, und
hörest du nicht,
Was Erlenkönig mir leise ver-
spricht?
Sei ruhig, bleibe ruhig, mein
Kind;
In dürren Blättern säuselt der
Wind.

"Willst, feiner Knabe, du mit mir
gehn?
Meine Töchter sollen dich warten
schön;
Meine Töchter führen den nächt-
lichen Reihn,
Und wiegen und tanzen und singen dich ein."

Mein Vater, mein Vater, und
siehst du nicht dort
Erlkönigs Töchter am düstern
Ort?

Who rides so late through night
and wind?
It is the father with his child.
He holds the boy tight in his
arms,
He clasps him safely, he keeps
him warm.

My son, why do you hide
your face so anxiously?
Do you not see the Erlking,
Father?
The Erlking with crown and
train?
My son, it is a streak of mist.

"You dear child, come with
me!
Truly lovely games I will play
with you;
Many colored flowers are on the
shore,
My mother has many golden
robes."

My father, my father, and don't
you hear,
What the Erlking softly promises
me?
Be quiet, stay quiet, my child;

It's the wind rustling in the dry
leaves.

"Will you go with me, fine boy?

My daughters will be waiting for
you eagerly;
My daughters lead the nightly
dance,
And whirl and dance and sing
when you come."

My father, my father, and don't
you see there
Erlking's daughter in the sha-
dowy place?

Mein Sohn, mein Sohn, ich seh'
es genau;
Es scheinen die alten Weiden so
grau.

"Ich liebe dich, mich reizt deine
schöne Gestalt;
Und bist du nicht willig, so
brauch' ich Gewalt."
Mein Vater, mein Vater, jetzt
fasst er mich an!
Erlkönig hat mir ein Leids getan!

Dem Vater grauset's, er reitet
geschwind,
Er hält in Armen das ächzende
Kind,
Erreicht den Hof mit Müh' und
Noth;
In seinen Armen das Kind war
tot.

My son, my son, I see it clearly;

The old willows appear so
grey.

"I love you, your lovely figure
delights me;
And if you aren't willing, I will
use force."
My father, my father, now he
seizes me!
Erlking has done me harm!

The father shudders, he rides
swiftly on,
He holds in his arms the groaning
child,
Reaches the courtyard with trou-
ble and difficulty;
In his arms the child was dead.

Johann Wolfgang von Goethe

trans. by Leon Plantinga

6c

SCHUBERT
Wandrers Nachtlied II, D.768 (1824)

Über allen Gipfeln	Over all the mountains peaks
Ist Ruh',	Is peace,
In allen Wipfeln	In all the treetops
Spürest du	You feel
Kaum einen Hauch;	Hardly a breath;
Die Vöglein schweigen im Walde.	The little birds keep silent in the woods.
Warte nur, balde	Only wait, soon
Ruhest du auch.	You too will rest.
Johann Wolfgang von Goethe	trans. by Leon Plantinga

6d

SCHUBERT
Auf dem Wasser zu singen, D.774 (1823)

Mitten im Schimmer der spie- gelnden Wellen Gleitet, wie Schwäne, der wan- kende Kahn; Ach, auf der Freude sanftschim- mernden Wellen Gleitet die Seele dahin wie der Kahn; Denn von dem Himmel herab auf die Wellen Tanzet das Abendroth rund um den Kahn.	Amid the shimmer of the mirror- ing waves Glides, like swans, the wavering boat; Ah, on the soft-shimmering waves of joy Glides the soul thence, like the boat; For down from heaven onto the waves Dances the sunset all 'round the boat.

Über den Wipfeln des westlichen
    Haines
Winket uns freundlich der röth-
    liche Schein;
Unter den Zweigen des östlichen
    Haines
Säuselt der Kalmus im röthlichen
    Schein;
Freude des Himmels und Ruhe
    des Haines
Athmet die Seel' im erröthenden
    Schein.

Ach, es entschwindet mit taui-
    gem Flügel
Mir auf den wiegenden Wellen
    die Zeit;
Morgen entschwinde mit schim-
    merndem Flügel
Wieder wie gestern und heute die
    Zeit;
Bis ich auf höherem strahlenden
    Flügel
Selber entschwinde der wech-
    selnden Zeit.

        Friedrich Leopold Stolberg

Over the treetops of the westerly
    grove
The reddish light beckons us;

Under the branches of the east-
    erly grove
The calamus rustles in the reddish
    light;
The joy of heaven and the peace
    of the grove
Breathes the soul in the redden-
    ing light.

Ah, time slips away on dewy
    wings
For me on the rocking waves;

Tomorrow may time slip away
    on shimmering wings
Again like yesterday and today;

Till I on brighter shining wings
Myself shall slip away to the
    changing time.

        trans. by Leon Plantinga

7

GIOACCHINO ROSSINI (1792–1868)
Il Barbiere di Siviglia (1816),
quintet from Act II

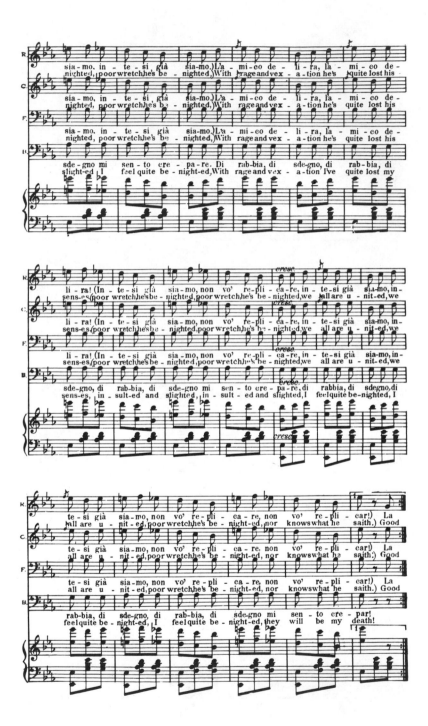

8

FRANZ LISZT (1811–86)
Overture to *Tannhäuser*, Concert
Paraphrase (1848)

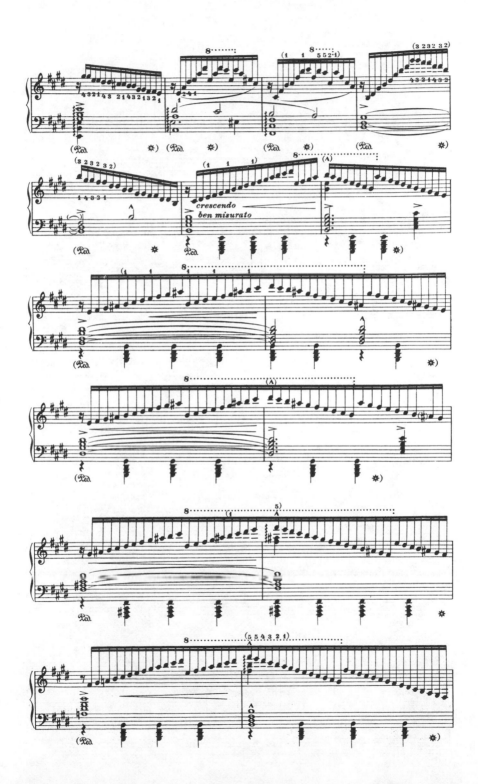

9

LISZT
Années de Pèlerinage, Part II, No. 1
(Sposalizio) (1838–39)

10

FRÉDÉRIC CHOPIN (1810–49)
Polonaise in C# Minor, Opus 26, No. 1
(1834–35)

Polonaise da Capo al Fine.

11

CHOPIN
Mazurkas, Opus 17 (1832–33), Nos. 1–4

12

CHOPIN
Ballade in G Minor, Opus 23 (1831–35)

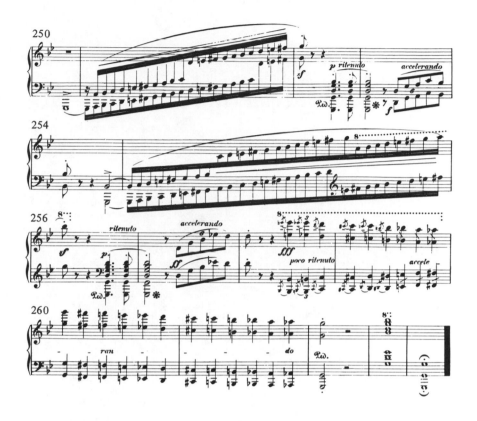

13

HECTOR BERLIOZ (1803–69)
La Damnation de Faust (1846), Scenes 16–20

Toi seu _ le   don _ nes trê _ ve   à mon en _ nui sans fin.
die ein _ zig   du ge _ wäh _ rest   Rast meinem ste _ ten Schmerz!
Un _ chang _ ing,   deathlessMoth _ er,   give me thine aid su _ preme!

chers!___ Tor_rents, pré_ci_pi_tez vos on _ _ _ des! A vos bruits sou_ve_rains
*Fels!___ Du Strom, lass dei_ne Wo_gen brau _ _ _ sen! Freudig sint sich mein Ruf_*
winds!___ Ye floods, roar with crash of thun _ _ _ der! Your wild an_ger and strife

88

Sur ces deux noirs chevaux,prompts com_me la pen_sé_e, Mon_tons, et au ga_lop! la jus_tice est pres_sé_e.
Stei_ge auf die_sesPferd,schnell fliegt es wie der Blitz. Und nun, fort im Ga_lopp, denn das Blut_gericht säumt nicht.
Mount on this jet black steed, ride on_ward fleet as the wind! A_way, swift as the wind, ere the law hath its ven_geance!

Faust et Méphistophélès galopant sur deux chevaux noirs.
Faust und Mephistopheles auf schwarzen Pferden daher brausend.
Faust and Mephistopheles on black steeds rush by.

69

Quels cris af_freux!
Hörst   du den Schrei?
I   hear them scream!

Ils me frap_pent de l'ai _ le!
Ih_reSchwingen mich peit _ schen!
With their pi_nions they beat   me!

(retenant son cheval)
(sein Ross bändigend)
(reining in his steed)

Le glas des tré_pas_
Die Todten_glo_cke
The deathbell soon you'll

90

*) Man kann die Horntöne forciren um Jagdklänge nachzuahmen. Dies bezeichnet der Ausdruck „cuivrer". Auf gestopfte Töne angewandt, er-
gibt es einen sehr seltsamen Effekt. — G è v a e r t, Instrumentationslehre.

Anmerkung der Herausgeber.

*) On peut forcer les sons du cor de façon à imiter la trompe de chasse; c'est ce qu'on appelle c u i v r e r les sons. Appliqué aux notes bou-
chées, cet effet est des plus étranges. — Gevaert, Traité d'instrumentation.

Note des éditeurs.

*) It is possible to so force the tone of the horn as to imitate that of the (French) hunting horn; this is to "cuivrer les sons" (make the notes
brassy). Applied to closed notes the effect is most weird. — G e v a e r t, Treatise on Instrumentation.

Editors' note.

95

100

114

117

Roulement par deux Timbaliers avec des baguettes d'éponge sur un Tamtam suspendu par sa courroie.
Il faut quelqu'un pour tenir le Tamtam en l'air pendant que les Timbaliers font leur roulement.
*2 Paukenschläger wirbeln auf einem an seinem Riemen aufgehängten Tamtam. Ein Mann hält das
Tamtam in der Luft, während die Paukenschläger wirbeln.*
2 kettle-drummers to beat a tamtam suspended by a strap. One man to hold up the tamtam while the
drummers beat it.

120

F. Il pleut du sang!...   (D'une voix tonnante.)
es reg-net Blut!...   (*Mit donnernder Stimme.*)
It raineth blood!...   (With thundering voice.)

M. Co _ hor _ tes in _ fer _ na _ les,   Son _ nez,   son _ nez vos
Der Höl _ le mächt' _ ge   Schaa _ ren,   lasst dröh _ nend eu _ re
Ye   powers of Hell tri _ umph _ ant!   Vic _ to _ rious trum _ pets

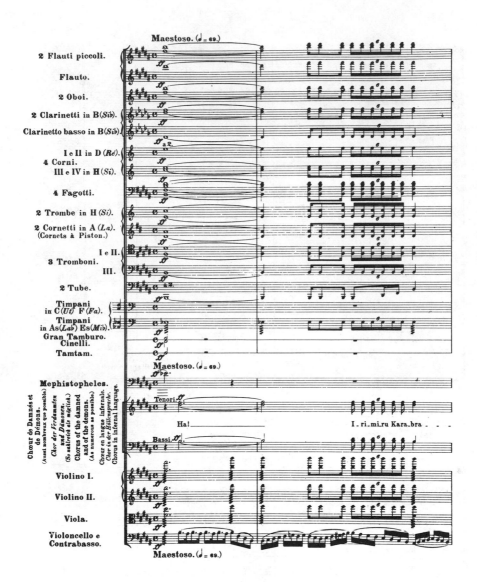

Il si ̱ gna li ̱ bre ̱ ment.
Er ward mein oh ̱ ne Zwang.
Yea, he will ̱ ing ̱ ly signed!

Si ̱ gné l'ac ̱ te fa ̱ tal qui le livre à nos flammes?
Faust den furcht ̱ ba ̱ ren Pakt, der ihn e ̱ wig ver ̱ dammet?
Yields he all   by the parchment which dooms him for   ev ̱ er?

43

di _ xé, Tru _ din _ xé ca _ ra _ i _ bo.   Mit ays _ ko, mé _ ron _ dor, mit ays _

Fir o _ me _ vi _ xé mé _ ron _ dor. Mit ays _ ko, mé _ ron _ dor, mit ays _

76

85

107

110

Si l'on peut avoir un chœur de deux ou trois cents enfants, il devra être placé derrière l'orchestre sur les gradins plus élevés que les instrumentistes. Il sera conduit par un maître de chant, et le chef d'orchestre, sans le voir, suivra de l'oreille son mouvement. Si l'on ne peut avoir qu'une trentaine de jeunes garçons, il faudra les disséminer derrière le chœur, sur l'avant-scène et dans l'orchestre. (Note de H. Berlioz.)

Wenn ein Chor von 2 bis 300 Kindern zur Verfügung steht, so muss er hinter dem Orchester auf einer höheren Stufe wie die Instrumentalisten aufgestellt werden. Er wird von einem Chormeister geleitet und der Dirigent, ohne ihn zu sehen, folgt im Tempo mit dem Gehör. Kann man nur ungefähr 30 Knaben haben, so müssen sie theils hinter dem Chor, theils im Orchester zerstreut aufgestellt werden.

If a chorus of 2 to 300 children can be got together, they must be placed behind the orchestra but raised so as to be higher than the instrumentalists. This chorus should be conducted by a chorus-master, and the conductor of the orchestra must follow him by ear, as he cannot see him. If only some 30 boys can he had, they must be placed apart, partly behind the chorus, partly in the orchestra.

3

Apothéose de Marguerite.
Margarethen's Verklärung.   Margherita's Apotheosis.

36

41

65

70

14

ROBERT SCHUMANN (1810–56)
from *Fantasiestücke,* Opus 12 (1837)

a. *Aufschwung*

b. *Warum?*

c. *Grillen*

d. *In der Nacht*

e. *Fabel*

15

SCHUMANN
from *Liederkreis,* Opus 39 (1840)

a. *In der Fremde*

Aus der Heimat hinter den
   Blitzen rot
Da kommen die Wolken her.
Aber Vater und Mutter sind
   lange tot,
Es kennt mich dort keiner mehr.

Wie bald, wie bald kommt die
   stille Zeit,
Da ruhe ich auch, und über mir
Rauschet die schöne Waldein-
   samkeit,
Und keiner kennt mich mehr
   hier.

From my homeland beyond the
   red lightning
There come the clouds over me,
But Father and Mother are long
   since dead
And no one there knows me any-
   more.

How soon, how soon, will come
   the quiet time,
When I rest too, and over me
Rustles the lovely, lonely woods

And no one here knows me any-
   more.

Joseph von Eichendorff   trans. by Leon Plantinga

b. *Intermezzo*

Dein Bildniss wunderselig
Hab' ich im Herzensgrund,
Das sieht so frisch und fröhlich
Mich an zu jeder Stund'.

Mein Herz still in sich singet
Ein altes schönes Lied,
Das in die Luft sich schwinget
Und zu dir eilig zieht.

    Joseph von Eichendorff

Your wonderfully blessed image
I keep in the bottom of my heart,
It looks so fresh and happily
At me at every hour.

My heart sings quietly to itself
An old, beautiful song,
That soars into the air
And hastens to you.

    trans. by Leon Plantinga

c. *Waldesgespräch*

Es ist schon spät, es ist schon kalt,	It is already late, it is already cold,
Was reit'st du einsam durch den Wald?	Why are you riding alone through the wood?
Der Wald ist lang, du bist allein,	The wood is vast, you are alone,
Du schöne Braut, ich führ' dich heim!	You pretty bride, I'll lead you home!

Gross ist der Männer Trug und List,	Great is men's deceit and cunning,
Vor Schmerz mein Herz gebrochen ist,	From pain my heart has broken,
Wohl irrt das Waldhorn her und hin,	The wandering hunting horn sounds here and there,
O fleih', du weisst nicht wer ich bin.	Oh flee, you do not know who I am.

So reich geschmückt ist Ross und Weib,	So richly adorned is horse and lady
So wunderschön der junge Leib;	So enchanting is your young body,
Jetzt kenn' ich dich, Gott steh' mir bei,	Now I know you—God be with me!
Du bist die Hexe Loreley!	You are the witch Lorelei!

Du kennst mich wohl, von hohem Stein	You know me indeed, from a high rock
Schaut still mein Schloss tief in den Rhein;	My castle looks silently deep into the Rhine;
Es ist schon spät, es ist schon kalt,	It is already late, it is already cold,
Kommst nimmermehr aus diesem Wald	You will nevermore leave this wood!

Joseph von Eichendorff   trans. by Leon Plantinga

d. *Die Stille*

Nicht schnell, immer sehr leise.

Es weiss und räth es doch Kei_ner, wie mir so wohl ist, so wohl! Ach!

wüsst' es nur Ei_ner, nur Ei_ner, kein Mensch es sonst wis_sen sollt'! So

still ist's nicht draussen im Schnee, so stumm und ver_schwie_gen sind die

Etwas lebhafter.

Ster_ne nicht in der Höh', als mei_ne Ge_danken sind.___ Ich wünscht', ich wär' ein

Vög_lein und zö_ge ü_ber das Meer, wohl ü_ber das Meer und weiter, bis

Es weiss und rät es doch keiner,	No one knows or guesses it,
Wie mir so wohl ist, so wohl!	How happy I am, so happy!
Ach! wüsst' es nur einer, nur einer,	Ah, if only the one knew, only the one
Kein Mensch es sonst wissen sollt'!	No other person need know.
So still ist's nicht draussen im Schnee,	It is not so quiet outside in the snow,
So stumm und verschwiegen sind	Not so dumb and silent
Die Sterne nicht in der Höh',	Are the stars on high,
Als meine Gedanken sind.	As are my thoughts.
Ich wünscht', ich wär' ein Vöglein	I wish I were a little bird
Und zöge über das Meer,	And could fly over the sea,
Wohl über das Meer und weiter,	Indeed over the sea and farther,
Bis dass ich im Himmel wär'.	Until I were in heaven!

Joseph von Eichendorff   trans. by Leon Plantinga

e. *Mondnacht*

Es war, als hätt' der Himmel
Die Erde still geküsst,
Dass sic im Blütenschimmer
Von ihm nur träumen müsst'.

Die Luft ging durch die Felder,

Die Aehren wogten sacht,
Es rauschten leis' die Wälder,
So sternklar war die Nacht.

Und meine Seele spannte
Weit ihre Flügel aus,
Flog durch die stillen Lande
Als flöge sie nach Haus.

Joseph von Eichendorff

It was as if heaven had
Quietly kissed the earth.
So that in glimmering blossoms
She must dream only of him.

The breeze went through the
    fields
The corn swayed softly
The woods rustled lightly
So clear and starry was the night.

And my soul spread
Wide her wings,
Flew through the silent land
As though she were flying home.

trans. by Leon Plantinga

16

FELIX MENDELSSOHN (1809–47)
St. Paul, Opus 36 (1836), Nos. 16–22

No. 16

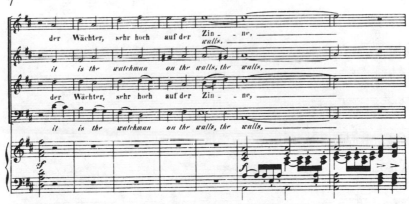

No. 17

No. 18

No. 19

No. 20

No. 21

No. 22

17

MENDELSSOHN
Piano Trio No. 1 in D Minor, Opus 49
(1839), third movement

18

RICHARD WAGNER (1813–83)
Die Walküre (1854–56), Act III, scene 3

447

fest mich bin - den, dem feig - sten Man - ne zur leich - ten Beu - te;   dies Ei - ne
fast shall bind me, for ba - sest cra - ven an ea - sy boot - y;   this one thing

452

musst du er - hö - ren,   was heil' - ge Angst   zu dir
must thou grant me   in deep - est an - guish I

457

fleht!   Die schla - fen - de schüt - ze mit scheu - chenden
pray: o shel - ter me sleep-ing with scar - ing

461

bestimmt
firmly

Schrecken, dass nur ein furcht - los frei - ester Held hier auf dem Fel - sen einst   mich
hor - rors, that but the first, most fear - less of he - roes e'er may find me here   on the

465

fänd!
fell!
WOTAN.

Zu - viel   be -
Too much   thou

(Sie schlägt das Haupt wieder zurück, und blickt, immer noch ihn umfassend,
(*She throws her head back again and still embracing Wotan, gazes with*
a tempo.

feierlich ergriffen Wotan in das Auge.)
deep enthusiasm in his eyes.)

647

zu liegen, über den sich eine breitästige Tanne ausstreckt.)
by a wide-spreading fir tree, and lays her upon it.)

(Er betrachtet sie und schliesst
(He looks upon her and closes

la melodia molto cantabile.
l'accompagnamento sempre legatissimo e dolcissimo.

651

ihr den Helm; sein Auge weilt dann auf der Gestalt der Schlafenden, die er nun mit dem grossen Stahlschilde der Walküren ganz
her helmet; his eyes then rest on the form of the sleeper, which he then completely covers with the great steel shield of the

655

zudeckt. ─ Langsam kehrt er sich ab, mit einem schmerzlichen Blicke wendet er sich noch einmal um.)
Valkyrie. ─ He turns slowly away, then again turns round with a sorrowful look.)

658

661

665

19

GIUSEPPE VERDI (1813–1901)
Otello (1887), Act III, scenes 1 and 2

Scene I.

Otello.

Araldo.

(dal peristilio, a Otello che sarà con Jago nella sala.)
(from the portico, to Otello who is with Iago in the hall.)

senza misura

La ve - det - ta del por-to ha se - gna-la - to la ve - ne - ta gu - le - a
Sir, the watch of the port has just sig-nalled the ar - ri - val of the gal - ley

ppp col canto

Scene II.

Allegro moderato. ♩= 72.

20

MODEST MUSORGSKY (1839–81)
Boris Godunov (1868–69), from "The Clapping Game" to the end of Act II

93 Vivo. ♩= 192.

Feod.

Ska-zoch - ka pro to i pro syo: kak ku-roch-ka bych-ka ro-di - la. Po-ro
I'll tell you a tale, and you'll laugh! How once a hen did hatch a fine calf, How a

syo - no-chek ya - ich - ko snyos. Skaz - ka po-yot-sya, dur-nyam ne da-yot - sya.
pig once laid a large white egg. Take it or leave it, All wise folk be - lieve it!

mf

cresc.

94 (He rises and stands in front of the Nurse. While singing, he claps his hands on the first beat of each bar.)

Tu - ru, tu - ru, pe - tu - shok, ty da - le - kol
Tou-rou, tou-rou lit - tle cock, Whith-er dost thou

f *dim.* *pp*

o - to - shol? Za mo-re, za mo - re, k ki - e - vu go - ro-du. Tam dub sto - it
go so far? To the sea, the blue sea, All the sights of Kiev to see. There an old oak

389

smert - nyi...   O, Gos - po - di, Bo - zhe moi!
haunts me...   O, God a_bove, save thou me!

Moderato assai. ♩= 84.

112   *Boris.*

Chto ta - ko - e?
What's this tu _ mult?

Nurses and Servants behind the Scenes.

Sopr.
Ai,   kysh!
Aï   Hsh!

Alti.

Moderato assai. ♩= 84.

112

(To his son, in anger)

Uz-
Go,

Ai,   kysh   kysh   Akh - ti!
Aï   hsh,   hoh!   Av, aï!

B Poco più mosso *(moderato).* ♩=92.

-li - kii go - su - dar! Te - be knyaz Va-si-lii Shui-skii che - lom byot.
Gracious lord and Tsar! It is Prince Vassily Shouïsky who craves an audience.

Bor.

Shui-skii?   Zo - vi!
Shouïsky?   Tis well!

Ska - zhi, chto ra - dy vi - det knya-zya i zhdyom ye-go be - se - dy.
Go, say his wish shall be ful - fill'd,   a - non we will hold con - verse.

113 *The Boyard in Waiting* (*The boyard rises and whispers in Boris' ear.*)

Ve - chor Push - ki - na kho - lop pri - shol sdo - no - som,
Last night from Poushkin came a serf who brought ill ti - dings

na shui - sko - go, Msti - slav - sko - go i pro - chikh, i na kho-zya - i - na:
the dis-tricts are o'er-run with re - bel boy-ards and no - bles in re - volt;

Feodor sits on his father's knee.

(Boris caresses him.)

net, di-tya! Vsyo, sly-shish, vsyo, kak by-lo.
Nay, my son! Tell me all. *See, I list-en.*

D Andantino. ♩=84.
Feod.
molto cantabile

Po-pin-ka nash si-del s mam-ka-mi v svet-li-tse, bez u-mol-ku bol-
Po-pin-ka, our old par-ra-keet set the maids laughing Chat-t'ring with-out a

-tal, ve-sel byl i las-kov. K mam-mush-kam pod-kho-dil, pro-sil che-sat go-lov-ku,
pause, Oh he was so fun-ny! Bend-ing his lit-tle head and ask-ing them to scratch it,

Poccissimo più mosso.

k kazh-doi on pod-kho-dil, che-ryod im so-blyu-da-ya. Mam-ka Na-sta-
Yes, ev'-ry one in turn, he made them all car-ess him. **E** *On-ly nurse Nas-*
ob.

-sya che-sat ne za-kho-te-la, Po-pin-ka, o-ser-dyas, naz-val mam-ku du-roi.
tas-ia would not pet or scratch him. Po-pin-ka in a rage used some shocking lan-guage.

118 L'istesso tempo. ♩ = 84.

me - ry,   sei zhe chas, chtob ot Lit - vy   Rus o - gra - di - las za - sta - va - mi,
steps,   lose no time, Let all the front - ier be protect - ed   at ev'. ry point,

chtob ni od - na du - sha ne - pe - re - shla za e - tu gran.   Stu - pai!   Net!
and see no liv. ing creature in . to Russ.ia pas.ses through!   Be .gone!   Nay,

cresc.

Adagio. ♩ = 56.

Po - stoi,   po - stoi, Shui - skii!   Sly - khal li ty ko-gda - ni - bud,   chtob
remain re - main, Shou'isky!   Hast ev . er heard men   tell   how

pp

de - ti myort - vy - e   iz gro-ba vy - kho - di - li,   do - pra - shi - vat tsa -
murd er'd babes a . rise from out their cof . fin'd slum . bers,   to vex the souls of

119

rei,   tsa-rei   za - kon - nykh,   iz - bran - nykh vse-na - rod - no, u -
Tsars,   of Tsars   and law . ful kings,   e . lect . ed by the peo . ple,   an .

ruch - ki i v pra - vol krep - ko szhav ig - rush - ku det - sku - yu...
fold - ed, but still he grasped the toy he last had play'd with.

Bor.

Do - vol - no!
En - ough, Prince!

(Boris makes a sign to dismiss Shouïsky. As the latter withdraws he glances back at Boris, who sinks into his arm chair.)

125 L'istesso tempo. ♩ = 72.

126
Recit.

Bor.   Tempo (*moderato*)

Uf!   tya - zhe - lo;   dai dukh pe - re - ve - du.   Ya
Ouf!   I suf - fo - cate! Scarce can I draw my breath!   I

chuv - sto - val: v sya krov mne ki - nu - las v lit - so i tyazh - ko o - pus -
feel that all my blood has rush'd in - to my brain; it stays there and still

Ye - di - no - e slu - chai - no za - ve - lo - sya,
some pet - ty and for - tu - i - tous dis - hon - our,

du - sha   sgo - rit,
at once   to prick,

na - lyot - sya serd   tse ya - dom,
and fill the heart   with poi - son.

tak   tyazh - ko,   tyazh - ko sta - net,
I   think   that   death   ap - proach - es,

chto   mo - lo - tom   stu - chit v u - shakh   u -
for   in mine ears   the pul - ses beat   like

-ko - rom   i   pro - klya - tem.   I
ham - mers   they beat   out   curs - es!   *My*

21

PYOTR IL'YICH TCHAIKOVSKY (1840–93)
Symphony No. 4 in F Minor, Opus 36
(1877), first movement

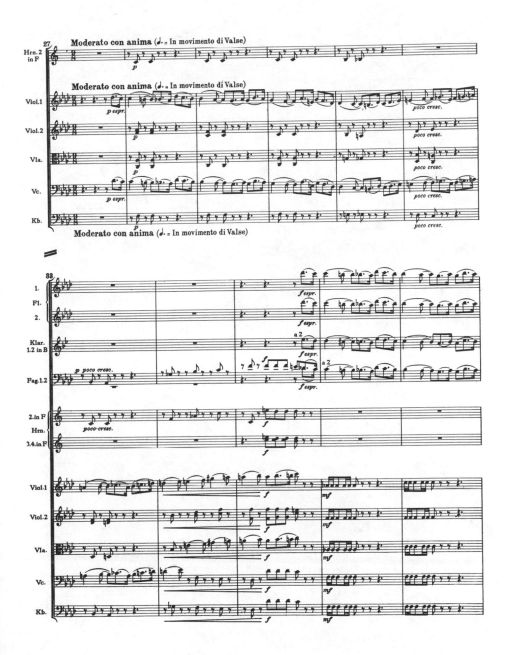

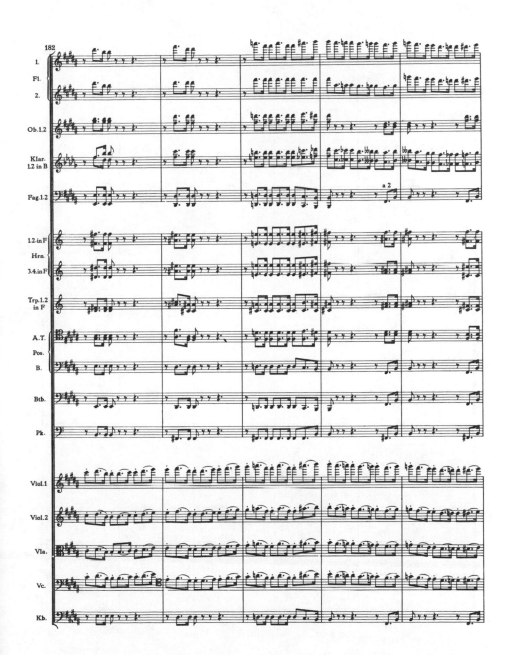

22

JOHANNES BRAHMS (1833–97)
Concerto for Violin in D Major, Opus 77
(1878), first movement

23

RICHARD STRAUSS (1864–1949)
Don Juan, Opus 20 (1888)

in E.
in E.
in E.
in E.
mit Holzschlägeln. Solo
pizz.
pizz.
pizz.
divisi

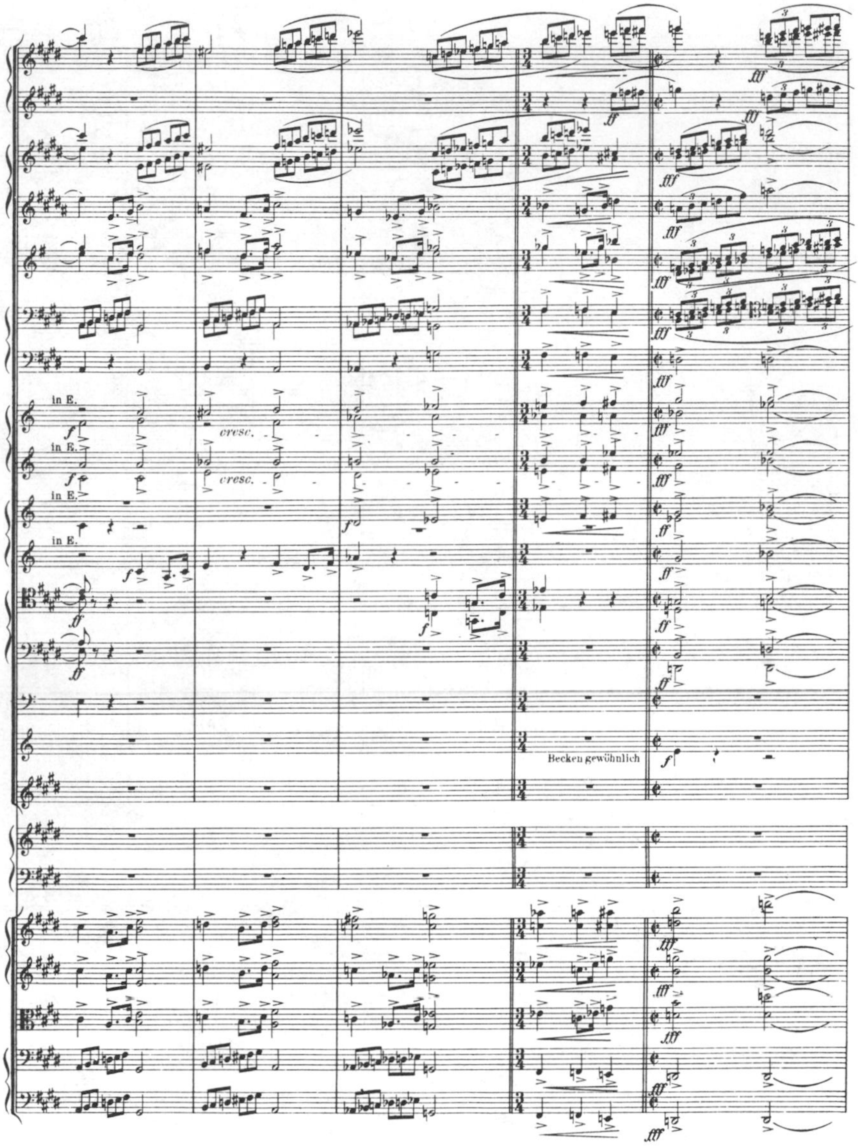
in E.
in E.
in E.
in E.
cresc.
cresc.
Becken gewöhnlich

*) Annerkung für den Dirigenten: Von hier *) bis *poco a poco calando* ganze Takte schlagen!

*) ganze Takte schlagen.

24

HUGO WOLF (1860–1903)
from *Mörike Lieder* (1888)

a. *Er ist's*

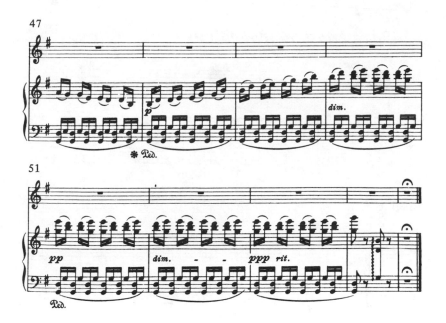

Frühling lässt sein blaues Band	Spring lets his blue ribbon
Wieder flattern durch die Lüfte;	Flutter again through the breezes;
Süsse, wohlbekannte Düfte	Sweet familiar smells
Streifen ahnungsvoll das Land.	Roam, full of hope, through the land.
Veilchen träumen schon,	Violets, already dreaming,
Wollen balde kommen.	Want to come out soon.
Horch, von fern ein leiser Har-	Listen, from afar the soft sound
fenton!	of a harp!
Frühling, ja du bist's!	Spring, yes it's you!
Dich hab' ich vernommen!	You I have perceived!

Eduard Mörike   trans. by Leon Plantinga

b. *Das verlassene Mägdlein*

Früh, wann die Hähne krähn,
Eh' die Sternlein schwinden,
Muss ich am Herde stehn,
Muss Feuer zünden.

Schön ist der Flammen Schein,
Es springen die Funken;
Ich schaue so darein,
In Leid versunken.

Plötzlich, da kommt es mir,
Treuloser Knabe,
Dass ich die Nacht von dir
Geträumet habe.

Träne auf Träne dann
Stürzet hernieder;
So kommt der Tag heran—
O ging' er wieder!

Early, when the cocks crow,
Before the little stars disappear,
I must be at the hearth,
Must light the fire.

Beautiful is the flames' light,
The sparks leap about;
I gaze into it,
Sunken in grief.

Suddenly it occurs to me,
Unfaithful boy,
That through the night of you
I dreamt.

Tear upon tear then
Tumbles down;
Thus the day begins,
Oh, would it were over!

Eduard Mörike   trans. by Leon Plantinga

c. *Um Mitternacht*

Gelassen stieg die Nacht ans Land,	Calmly night has gone ashore,
Lehnt trümend an der Berge Wand,	Leans, dreaming, against the mountain wall,
Ihr Auge sieht die goldne Waage nun	Her eye now sees the golden balance
Der Zeit in gleichen Schalen stille ruhn;	Of time, its scales even, quietly at rest;
Und kecker rauschen die Quellen hervor,	And more boldly the springs rush out,
Sie singen der Mutter, der Nacht, ins Ohr	They sing in the ear of the night, their mother
Vom Tage,	Of the day,
Vom heute gewesenen Tage	Of the day that has been today.

Das uralt alte Schlummerlied,	The ancient old lullaby
Sie achtet's nicht, sie ist es müd;	She disregards it, she is tired of it;
Ihr klingt des Himmels Bläue süsser noch,	To her the blue of heaven sounds still sweeter,
Der flücht'gen Stunden gleich-geschwungnes Joch.	The evenly-shared yoke of the fleeting hours.
Doch immer behalten die Quellen das Wort,	But still the springs keep speaking,
Es singen die Wasser im Schlafe noch fort	The water sings on in its sleep loudly
Vom Tage,	Of the day,
Vom heute gewesenen Tage.	Of the day that has been today.

Eduard Mörike   trans. by Leon Plantinga

d. *Seufzer*

Dein Liebesfeuer, ach Herr!	Your love fire, ah Lord!
Wie teuer wollt' ich es hegen,	How dearly I wanted to cherish it,
Wollt' ich es pflegen!	Wanted to protect it!
Hab's nicht geheget	I did not cherish it,
Und nicht gepfleget,	And did not protect it,
Bin tot im Herzen,	I am dead in my heart,
O Höllenschmerzen!	O pain of hell!

Eduard Mörike   trans. by Leon Plantinga

Appendix A

READING AN ORCHESTRAL SCORE

CLEFS

The music for some instruments is written in clefs other than the familiar treble and bass. In the following example, middle C is shown in the four clefs used in orchestral scores:

Treble clef   Alto clef   Tenor clef   Bass clef

The *alto clef* is primarily used in viola parts. The *tenor clef* is employed for cello, bassoon, and trombone parts when these instruments play in a high register.

TRANSPOSING INSTRUMENTS

The music for some instruments is customarily written at a pitch different from their actual sound. The following list, with examples, shows the main transposing instruments and the degree of transposition.

Instrument	Transposition	Written Note	Actual Sound
Piccolo Celesta	sound an octave higher than written		
Trumpet in F	sound a fourth higher than written		
Trumpet in E	sound a major third higher than written		
Clarinet in E♭ Trumpet in E♭	sound a minor third higher than written		
Trumpet in D Clarinet in D	sound a major second higher than written		

Clarinet in B♭
  Trumpet in B♭
  Cornet in B♭
  Horn in B♭ alto
	sound a major second
	lower than written	

Clarinet in A
  Trumpet in A
  Cornet in A
	sound a minor third
	lower than written	

Horn in G Alto flute	sound a fourth lower than written	
English horn Horn in F	sound a fifth lower than written	
Horn in E	sound a minor sixth lower than written	
Horn in E♭	sound a major sixth lower than written	
Horn in D	sound a minor seventh lower than written	

Contrabassoon
  Horn in C
  Double bass
	sound an octave
	lower than written	

Bass clarinet in B♭ (written in treble clef)	sound a major ninth lower than written	
(written in bass clef)	sound a major second lower than written	
Bass clarinet in A (written in treble clef)	sound a minor tenth lower than written	
(written in bass clef)	sound a minor third lower than written	

Appendix B

INSTRUMENTAL NAMES AND ABBREVIATIONS

The following tables set forth the English, Italian, German, and French names used for the various musical instruments in these scores, and their respective abbreviations. A table of the foreign-language names for scale degrees and modes is also provided.

Woodwinds

English	Italian	German	French
Piccolo (Picc.)	Flauto piccolo (Fl. Picc.)	Kleine Flöte (Kl. Fl.)	Petite flûte
Flute (Fl.)	Flauto (Fl.); Flauto grande (Fl. gr.)	Grosse Flöte (Fl. gr.)	Flûte (Fl.)
Alto flute	Flauto contralto (fl.c-alto)	Altflöte	Flûte en sol
Oboe (Ob.)	Oboe (Ob.)	Hoboe (Hb.); Oboe (Ob.)	Hautbois (Hb.)
English horn (E. H.)	Corno inglese (C. or Cor. ingl., C.i.)	Englisches Horn (E. H.)	Cor anglais (C. a.)
Sopranino clarinet	Clarinetto piccolo (clar. picc.)		
Clarinet (C., Cl., Clt., Clar.)	Clarinetto (Cl. Clar.)	Klarinette (Kl.)	Clarinette (Cl.)
Bass clarinet (B. Cl.)	Clarinetto basso (Cl. b., Cl. basso, Clar. basso)	Bass Klarinette (Bkl.)	Clarinette basse (Cl. bs.)
Bassoon (Bsn., Bssn.)	Fagotto (Fag., Fg.)	Fagott (Fag., Fg.)	Basson (Bssn.)
Contrabassoon (C. Bsn.)	Contrafagotto (Cfg., C. Fag., Cont. F.)	Kontrafagott (Kfg.)	Contrebasson (C. bssn.)

631

BRASS

English	Italian	German	French
French horn (Hr., Hn.)	Corno (Cor., C.)	Horn (Hr.) [*pl.* Hörner (Hrn.)]	Cor; Cor à pistons
Trumpet (Tpt., Trpt., Trp., Tr.)	Tromba (Tr.)	Trompete (Tr., Trp.)	Trompette (Tr.)
Trumpet in D	Tromba piccola (Tr. picc.)		
Cornet	Cornetta	Kornett	Cornet à pistons (C. à p., Pist.)
Trombone (Tr., Tbe., Trb., Trm., Trbe.)	Trombone [*pl.* Tromboni (Tbni., Trni.)]	Posaune (Ps., Pos.)	Trombone (Tr.)
Tuba (Tb.)	Tuba (Tb, Tba.)	Tuba (Tb.) [*also* Basstuba (Btb.)]	Tuba (Tb.)

PERCUSSION

English	Italian	German	French
Percussion (Perc.)	Percussione	Schlagzeug (Schlag.)	Batterie (Batt.)
Kettledrums (K. D.)	Timpani (Timp., Tp.)	Pauken (Pk.)	Timbales (Timb.)
Snare drum (S. D.)	Tamburo piccolo (Tamb. picc.) . Tamburo militare (Tamb. milit.)	Kleine Trommel (Kl. Tr.)	Caisse claire (C. cl.), Caisse roulante Tambour militaire (Tamb. milit.)
Bass drum (B. drum)	Gran cassa (Gr. Cassa, Gr. C., G. C.)	Grosse Trommel (Gr. Tr.)	Grosse caisse (Gr. c.)
Cymbals (Cym., Cymb.)	Piatti (P., Ptti., Piat.)	Becken (Beck.)	Cymbales (Cym.)
Tam-Tam (Tam-T.)			
Tambourine (Tamb.)	Tamburino (Tamb.)	Schellentrommel, Tamburin	Tambour de Basque (T. de B., Tamb. de Basque)
Triangle (Trgl., Tri.)	Triangolo (Trgl.)	Triangel	Triangle (Triang.)
Glockenspiel (Glocken.)	Campanelli (Cmp.)	Glockenspiel	Carillon
Bells (Chimes)	Campane (Cmp.)	Glocken	Cloches

Antique Cymbals	Crotali Piatti antichi	Antiken Zimbeln	Cymbales antiques
Sleigh Bells	Sonagli (Son.)	Schellen	Grelots
Xylophone (Xyl.)	Xilofono	Xylophon	Xylophone
Cowbells		Herdenglocken	

Crash cymbal	Grande cymbale chinoise
Siren	Sirène
Lion's roar	Tambour à corde
Slapstick	Fouet
Wood blocks	Blocs chinois

STRINGS

English	*Italian*	*German*	*French*
Violin (V., Vl., Vln, Vi.)	Violino (V., Vl., Vln.)	Violine (V., Vl., Vln.) Geige (Gg.)	Violon (V., Vl., Vln.)
Viola (Va., Vl., *pl.* Vas.)	Viola (Va., Vla.) *pl.* Viole (Vle.)	Bratsche (Br.)	Alto (A.)
Violoncello, Cello (Vcl., Vc.)	Violoncello (Vc., Vlc., Vcllo.)	Violoncell (Vc., (Vlc.)	Violoncelle (Vc.)
Double bass (D. Bs.)	Contrabasso (Cb., C. B.) *pl.* Contrabassi or Bassi (C. Bassi, Bi.)	Kontrabass (Kb.)	Contrebasse (C. B.)

OTHER INSTRUMENTS

English	*Italian*	*German*	*French*
Harp (Hp., Hrp)	Arpa (A., Arp.)	Harfe (Hrf.)	Harpe (Hp.)
Piano	Pianoforte (P.-f., Pft.)	Klavier	Piano
Celesta (Cel.)			
Harpsichord	Cembalo	Cembalo	Clavecin
Harmonium (Harmon.)			
Organ (Org.)	Organo	Orgel	Orgue
Guitar		Gitarre (Git.)	
Mandoline (Mand.)			

NAMES OF SCALE DEGREES AND MODES

SCALE DEGREES

English	Italian	German	French
C	do	C	ut
C-sharp	do diesis	Cis	ut dièse
D-flat	re bemolle	Des	ré bémol
D	re	D	ré
D-sharp	re diesis	Dis	ré dièse
E-flat	mi bemolle	Es	mi bémol
E	mi	E	mi
E-sharp	mi diesis	Eis	mi dièse
F-flat	fa bemolle	Fes	fa bémol
F	fa	F	fa
F-sharp	fa diesis	Fis	fa dièse
G-flat	sol bemolle	Ges	sol bémol
G	sol	G	sol
G-sharp	sol diesis	Gis	sol dièse
A-flat	la bemolle	As	la bémol
A	la	A	la
A-sharp	la diesis	Ais	la dièse
B-flat	si bemolle	B	si bémol
B	si	H	si
B-sharp	si diesis	His	si dièse
C-flat	do bemolle	Ces	ut bémol

MODES

major	maggiore	dur	majeur
minor	minore	moll	mineur

Appendix C

GLOSSARY

This glossary includes only terms found in this anthology. One common form of a word is given; the reader can easily deduce the meaning of its variations. Omitted are foreign terms very similar to English ones ("delicatamente") or in common use ("solo"). Please refer to Appendix B for names of musical instruments.

a. To, at, with.
accelerando. Becoming faster.
accentato. Accented.
accompagnamento. Accompaniment.
adagio. Slow, leisurely.
ad libitum. At the discretion of the performer.
agitato. Agitated, excited.
alla breve. In duple time, i.e., the half note rather than the quarter note is the basic unit.
allargando. Becoming broader.
allegretto. A moderately fast tempo (between allegro and andante).
allegro. A rapid tempo (between allegretto and presto).
allmälich. Gradually.
andante. A moderately slow tempo (between adagio and allegretto).
andantino. A tempo usually played slightly faster than andante.
Anfang. Beginning.
animato. Animated.
appassionato. Impassioned.
arco. Played with the bow.
ardito. Bold.
armonioso. Harmoniously.
arpeggiando. Played in harp style, i.e., the notes of a chord played in quick succession rather than simultaneously.
assai. Very.
ausdrucksvoll. With expression.

battute. Beat, rhythm.
belebt. Animated.
ben. Very.
bewegt. Agitated.
bisbigliando. Soft tremolo on the harp.
breit. Broadly.
brio. Vivacity.

cadenza. An improvisatory solo passage.
calando. Diminishing in volume and speed.
cantabile. In a singing style.
col canto; col parte. An indication that the accompaniment should follow the lead of the voice *(canto)* or soloist *(parte).*
come. As.
comincio. Beginning.
con. With.
corda. String.
crescendo. Becoming louder.
cupo. Hollow.

da capo. Repeat from the beginning.
dal segno al fine. Repeat from the sign to the end.
decrescendo. Becoming softer.
diminuendo. Becoming softer.
disperazione. Despair.
divisi. Divided (i.e., the group of instruments should be divided into parts to play the passage in question).

dolce. Sweet, gentle.
dreifach. Triple.
Dreitaktig. In phrases of three.
due. Two.
duolo. Grief.

einfach. Simple.
ersterbend. Dying away.
erstes. First.
espressivo. Expressive.
estremamente. Extremely.
etwas. Somewhat.

facile. easy.
feroce. Ferocious.
feurig. Fiery.
fine. End.
flebile. Feeble.
forza. Force.
fuoco. Fire, spirit.

ganz. Entirely.
garbo. Grace.
geschwind. Quick.
gestopt. Stopped.
geteilt. Same as "divisi" (cf. above).
getragen. Sustained.
gewöhnlich. Usual.
giocoso. Jocose.
giusto. Moderate.
glissando. Gliding quickly over successive notes.
grazioso. Graceful.

Hälfte. Half.
heftig. Intense.
heimlich. Furtively.

immer. Always.
innig. Intimate.
istesso tempo. Same tempo.

jubelnd. Jubilant.

kleine. Little.

langsam. Slow.
largo. A very slow tempo.
lebhaft. Lively.
legato. Smooth.
leggiero. Light and graceful.
Leidenschaft. Passion.
leise. Soft.
lento. A slow tempo, between andante and largo.
lunga. Long, sustained.
lusingando. Caressing.
lusinghiero. Alluring

m.d. Mano dextra (It.) or *main droit* (Fr.). Right hand.
m.g. Main gauche (Fr.). Left hand.
m.s. Mano sinistra (It.). Left hand.
ma. But.
maestoso. Majestic.
marcato. With emphasis.
mässig. Moderate.
meno. Less.
mesto. Sad.
mezza voce. Only moderately loud (lit. "half-voice")
misura. Measure, beat.
misurato. Measured, moderate.
moderato. At a moderate tempo.
molto. Very, much.
morendo. Dying away.
mosso. Rapid.
moto. Motion.
movimento. Motion.
muta. Change (tuning or instrument).

nach und nach. More and more.
nicht. Not.

ordinario. In the ordinary way (cancelling a special instruction).
ossia. An alternative passage.

patetico. With great emotion.
pausa. Rest.
per. By, through.
perdendosi. Gradually dying away.
pesante. Heavily.
a piacere. At the discretion of the performer.

piacevole. Pleasing.

più. More.

pizzicato. Plucked (the string plucked by the finger).

pochissimo. Very little.

poco. Little.

poco a poco. Little by little.

ponticello. Bridge (of a stringed instrument).

precipitato. Impetuously, rushed.

presto. A very quick tempo (faster than allegro).

prima. First.

quasi. Almost, as if.

quattro. Four.

rallentando. Becoming slower.

rasch. Quick.

recitative. A singing style imitating speech.

rinforzando. Emphasis on a note or chord.

risoluto. Determined, resolute.

ritardando. Slowing.

ritenuto. Holding back in speed.

ritmo. Rhythm.

ruhig. Calm.

sfz., sf (sforzando). With sudden emphasis.

scherzando. Playfully,

schleppen. Dragging.

schmerzlich. Sad.

schnell. Fast.

sehr. Very.

semplice. In a simple manner.

sempre. Always.

senza. Without.

simile. In a similar manner.

smorzando Dying away.

soffocata. Choking.

sordino. Mute.

sostenuto. Sustained.

sotto voce. In an undertone.

sprechend. Spoken.

staccato. Suddenly detached.

stesso. Same.

stretto. Increasing speed (of a concluding section of a non-fugal work).

stringendo. Quickening.

subito. Suddenly.

sul; sur. On.

tenuto. Held, sustained.

tre. Three.

tremolo. Rapid reiteration of one or more notes.

trill. Rapid alternation of a note with the note a second above.

troppo. Too much.

tutti. All.

umstimmen. To change the tuning.

una. One.

und. And.

ursprünglich. Initially.

valse. Waltz.

veloce. Fast.

vierfach. Into four parts.

vivace. Lively.

vivamente. vivaciously.

vivo. Lively.

voce. Voice.

weich. Smooth.

wie. As.

zart. Delicately.

ziemlich. Suitable.

zu. At.

zurückhaltend. Slackeniung in speed.

zweitaktig. In phrases of two.